WHAT WE CALL A HOUSE, OR A PLACE OF WORSHIP, OR A PLACE TO WORK IN OR A PLACE TO DANCE IN OR SING IN, WELL SUCH PLACES CANNOT EXIST AT ALL AS ANY FORM OF LIFE UNLESS THEY ARE INTERPRETATIONS OF HUMAN LIFE. THEY EXPRESS AND BLESS THE HUMAN BEINGS.

—FRANK LLOYD WRIGHT "ARCHITECTURE AND MODERN LIFE: DIALOGUE," 1939

FRANK LLOYD WRIGHT'S
PUBLIC BUILDINGS

⊞ CARLA LIND ⊞

AN ARCHETYPE PRESS BOOK
POMEGRANATE ARTBOOKS, SAN FRANCISCO

Library of Congress Cataloging-in-Publication Data

Lind, Carla.

Frank Lloyd Wright's public buildings / Carla Lind.

       p.   cm.   — (Wright at a glance)

"An Archetype Press book."

Includes bibliographical references.

ISBN 0-7649-0016-1 (hc)

1. Public buildings — United States. 2. Organic architecture — United States. 3. Architecture, Modern — 20th century — United States. 4. Wright, Frank Lloyd, 1867–1959 — Criticism and interpretation. I. Title. II. Series: Lind, Carla. Wright at a glance.

NA 4208.L56 1996   96-18139

720'.92—dc20   CIP

Published by

Pomegranate

Box 808022

Petaluma, California

94975-8022

Catalogue no. A861

Produced by Archetype Press, Inc.

Project Director: Diane Maddex

Editorial Assistants:

Gretchen Smith Mui and Kristi Flis

Designer: Robert L. Wiser

10 9 8 7 6 5 4 3 2

Printed in Singapore

Opening photographs:
Page 1: Frank Lloyd Wright in 1953 explaining the Unitarian Meeting House (1947). Page 2: Guggenheim Museum (1943–59). Pages 6–7: Annunciation Greek Orthodox Church (1956).

CONTENTS

FRANK LLOYD WRIGHT'S VISIONARY architectural theories were not confined to dwellings but encompassed all of society's needs as well. Wright (1867–1959) was driven by a desire that America's architecture reflect the uniqueness of its democratic lifestyle, its natural and technological resources, and its free spirit. He called it "building for democracy."

Although the vast majority of Wright's commissions were for residences and their related outbuildings, he provided revolutionary designs for a broad range of nonresidential buildings, entire communities, and even airplane hangers and automobiles. Most were never built, unable as he was to break through bureaucracies or overcome the traditional tastes and budgets of ruling committees. Wright was far more successful in persuading an individual or a family to accept his unconventional ideas. Completed buildings serving public needs thus usually resulted from strong leaders who believed in him and fought hard to see the projects through to completion.

Only ninety of Wright's public buildings were

Wright's last public building to be built was the Gammage Memorial Auditorium (1959) at Arizona State University in Tempe. The theater's spherical theme travels from its scalloped concrete roof to globe lights along the walkway.

Wright left his mark on places close to him: In Richland Center, Wisconsin, his birthplace, he designed the innovative German Warehouse in 1915 (opposite). Oak Park, Illinois, has erected a replica of his 1909 Horse Show Fountain (above).

erected, their functions ranging from medical clinics to sporting clubs; schools, libraries, and museums to retail shops and banks; government buildings to corporate offices; theaters to churches; even a gas station, warehouse, and railway waiting station. He also designed smaller structures: fountains, sculptures, and bridges. No aspect of life was beyond his interest.

Wright's acceptance as an architect of commercial, religious, and community buildings increased significantly after the acclaimed Johnson Wax Administration Building was completed in 1939. Half of his public buildings were built in the last twenty years of his seventy-year career, when many of his unbuilt masterpieces, such as the Rogers Lacy Hotel (1946), Lenkurt Electric Company (1955), and Arizona State Capitol (1957), were also designed.

The scale of his larger projects opened up new challenges to Wright's creativity, which similarly challenged the public's imagination. The prophetic National Life Insurance skyscraper, designed in 1924, and the awe-inspiring "Mile High" skyscraper he offered to Chicago in 1956 have not been built, but construction of

A small essay resembling
his spiraling design for the
Guggenheim Museum, the
Anderton Court Shops (1952)
stand out even amid the
opulent wares on Rodeo Drive
in Beverly Hills. Shoppers
wend their way up a ramp
crowned by a serrated spire.

the Monona Terrace Civic Center, designed for Madison, Wisconsin, in 1938, was finally begun in 1995 after fifty-seven controversial years.

According to his tenets of organic architecture, Wright studied the client and the life that was to take place within each building: worshiping, working, governing, playing, or learning. He then sought a unique design solution that grew from this function, the site, and the materials available. Again and again, it was the space within each building that called out the facade. In each creation Wright was celebrating democracy and the sovereignty of the individual.

Wright's public buildings represent only eighteen percent of his executed designs, but they are a disproportionate one-third of his demolished works. Only sixty structures survive, with most of the losses occurring in recreation—clubs, restaurants, hotels—an industry especially subject to fashion. But unlike private houses, the relative accessibility of the public buildings that remain continues to enable countless persons to witness the artful spaces of America's most renowned architect.

Organic architecture

Focused on the space within each building and how a building fulfills the client's needs

Innovative uses of technology

New systems challenging the innate qualities of building components to achieve design goals. Innovations such as experimental lighting, glass tubes, and prism glass

Generous use of concrete, glass, and steel

Larger commissions calling for more durable, stronger materials than wood, a feature of many of Wright's houses

Integral ornament

Multiple arts unified into each design, with the building materials and forms themselves providing added decorative details

Organic siting

Design concepts based on both limitations and strengths of the site

Common grammar

A design theme for each building, used consistently to create visual unity throughout the structure

Powerful geometric shapes

Bolder than residences because of the larger scale

Shift from rectilinear to circular forms

Greater use of curves, replacing angles from earlier in his career

Unity and harmony

All design elements working together to create a unique whole

Inward turning

Orientation toward an inner court to bring light inside, with few openings at eye level

Integral furnishings

Modular designs composed on a unit system. Custom-designed furnishings to suit the client, including innovative office chairs and desks

Human scale

Efforts to achieve spaces comfortable for human occupants despite the larger building size

More controversial projects

Public officials generally less cooperative than residential clients, resulting in some unbuilt projects

Top: Circular motifs at Johnson Wax (1936) and the Marin County Civic Center (1957). Bottom: Large-scale geometrics at the German Warehouse (1915) and Florida Southern College (1938).

UNITY TEMPLE

OAK PARK, ILLINOIS. 1904

WHEN THE OLD UNITARIAN CHURCH in Oak Park burned, Wright, a local architect with close ties to the church, was called on to create a new building. The limited budget, noisy location, and dual-purpose needs guided Wright in creating a structure devoid of any resemblance to a traditional steepled church.

Concrete, poured in place in forms repeated on each side, was the economical building method selected. The two parts of the design, one for worship and one for social services, were connected by a central entry hall. The worship space was entered through a lower cloister, which opened to a central seating area surrounded by balconies.

Secular activities were assigned to Unity House, centered on a large fireplace. The eighty-four-foot-long space was broken into galleries that could be divided into classrooms or used together for larger functions.

Wright placed soft greens, golds, and grays as artfully on the walls as they would have been in a two-dimensional painting, working with the lines and cubist forms of the church to create a three-dimensional sculpture.

Beneath flat roofs, solid walls rise to clerestory windows, shielding worshipers from outside distractions. In a lyrical tribute to concrete—soon to become one of his favorite materials—Wright made stylized plant forms grow on the church's columns.

· **17**

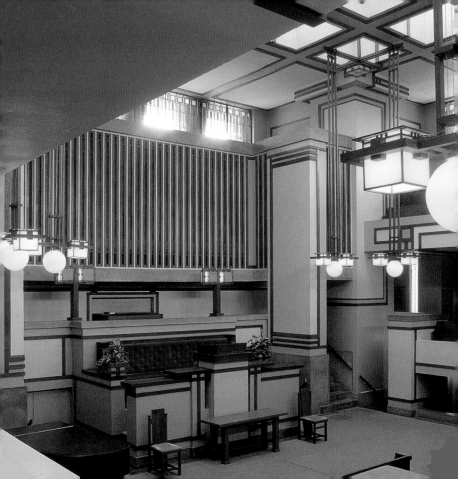

⊞ The building is an example of freedom based upon reason. . . . Its religious character is to be tested not by its resemblance to other churches but by its possession of the qualities of reverence, dignity and aspiration which belong to a house of worship. ⊞

Pastor Rodney Johonnot
*The New Edifice
of Unity Church,* 1906

Art glass skylights in the coffered ceiling repeat the rectilinear designs of wood banding on the surrounding walls and invite diffused light to enter from above. Cubes and spheres of artificial light add to the sublime effect.

ROOKERY REMODELING

The lobby was remodeled again in 1931 by Wright's former associate William Drummond, who all but obliterated the collaboration of the first two designers, Root and Wright. Restoration in 1990 principally replaced the Wright design, mixed with elements of Drummond's work and a few adaptations to meet current building needs.

▓ The fine-art sense of the profession was at that time practically dead; only glimmerings were perceptible in the work of Richardson and Root. ▓
Frank Lloyd Wright
"In the Cause of Architecture,"
Architectural Record, 1908

EARLY IN HIS CAREER WRIGHT WAS called on to remodel several commercial spaces. All had been lost to later remodelings until the largest, the whimsical lobby of the Rookery Building, was recently restored.

The original building was designed by Burnham and Root in 1886 but was considered too ornamental by 1905. Edward C. Waller, a Wright client who managed the building, commissioned Wright to simplify the design of the lobby and large central court with a glazed ceiling. Wright, whose office had been in the building six years earlier, replaced much of the elaborate ornamental ironwork with simpler geometric designs and resurfaced many pillars and planes in off-white marble. The dramatic staircases were terminated with his geometric flat urns. New circle-within-a-square bronze and glass light fixtures were suspended from the trusswork above.

Uncharacteristically, Wright decorated nearly all the marble surfaces with incised gold arabesque designs, probably because of his respect for John Wellborn Root and his geometric designs. He also retained the mosaic tile floor and Root's masterful spatial relationships.

JOHNSON WAX BUILDINGS

Giant lily-pad piers support the Administration Building, which is capped by a tubular glass cornice and ceiling in the main workroom. Throughout, custom red tubular steel furniture with the same curvilinear forms as the building creates a composed harmony.

THE SUCCESS OF WRIGHT'S RENOWNED designs for S. C. Johnson and Son was a tribute to his relationship with the client, Herbert Johnson, and his associate Jack Ramsey. Their faith in the seventy-year-old architect and their shared vision of a truly American office building responsive to the needs of the workers enabled Wright to create a pivotal masterpiece that would reinvigorate his tired career and open new horizons.

The beauty of the two Johnson buildings lies in Wright's approach to workspaces. As in the Larkin Building (1904), Wright sought to protect the workers in the Administration Building from its industrial site and turned the building inward, with diffused light entering from above. He thus dematerialized the boxiness of traditional buildings, freeing walls and interior spaces.

In the adjoining Research Tower, another engineering feat built a decade later, tubular glass walls wrap the fifteen stories. Reinforced concrete floors cantilever from the central core like branches from a tree, clad with brick. Polished red floors, shiny brass railings, and red brick walls in the sculpted spaces glow with warmth.

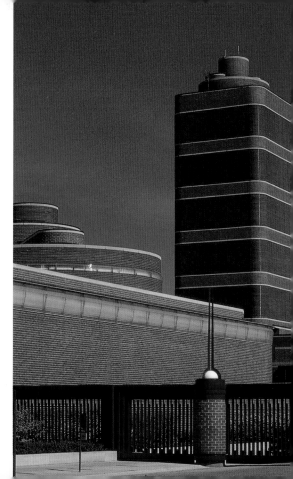

▓▓ It may be argued that Wright's Administration Building for Johnson Wax is not only the greatest piece of twentieth century architecture realized in the United States to date but also possibly the most profound work of art that America has ever produced. ▓▓

Kenneth Frampton
In *Frank Lloyd Wright and the Johnson Wax Buildings*, 1986

Streamlined circular forms undulate throughout the complex: from the low spirals of the earlier Administration Building to the rounded corners of the Research Tower, whose walls melt in glass.

Wright's unique system of translucent Pyrex glass tubing encourages natural light into the Administration Building. When night falls, bulbs simulate the effect of the sun. The rounded, horizontal tubes were a perfect match for the sleek lines of the building.

FLORIDA SOUTHERN COLLEGE

LAKELAND, FLORIDA. 1938-54

Cantilevered concrete esplanades link campus buildings and provide relief from the southern sun. The chapel's tower rises over all, the focal point of the institution.

THE INDIVIDUAL WHO HAD THE vision and confidence in Wright to make the Florida Southern College campus a reality was its president, Ludd M. Spivey. He sought Wright as much for his philosophy as for his architecture. According to their master plan, a complex of twelve Wright structures would be constructed over a twenty-year period in a gardenlike setting overlooking a lake in a former orange grove.

Wright loved being around young people and called for student participation. Using local materials—Tidewater cypress and cast-concrete blocks rich with sand and crushed shells—they created truly indigenous and imaginative forms. The buildings used a diagonal scheme of thirty- and sixty-degree angles and were connected by esplanades made of the concrete block.

The first building to be constructed was the Annie Merner Pfeiffer Chapel in 1938. Its hexagonal plan with rectangular extensions on either side created a theater-like setting lighted by large windows and a skylight. A distinctive bell tower rises above, repeating the school's thematic angular forms on a vertical plane.

Inside the chapel, a delicate
roof of glass reaches steeple-
like toward the sky, while
the choir loft is screened by
a geometric concrete lattice.
Sections of the building's
lower block are pierced to
allow light to enter through
tiny facets of colored glass.

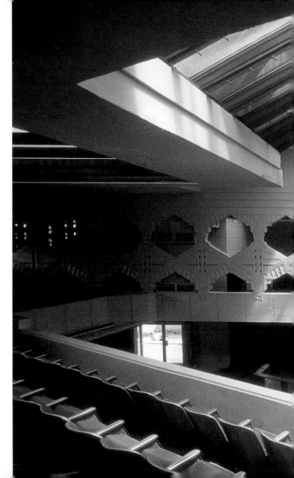

UNITARIAN MEETING HOUSE

SHOREWOOD HILLS, WISCONSIN. 1947

In an appearance on the "Today" show in 1953, Wright demonstrated the triangular shape of the church's roof as a fitting complement to the building's triangular plan. The shape, he explained, created the "expression of reverence without recourse to the steeple."

FRANK LLOYD WRIGHT, A UNITARIAN rooted in the traditions of the church, was a natural selection for the sixty-year-old First Unitarian Society. The inspiring result was a collective effort to which members, contractors, and architect all volunteered. For five years they struggled—physically, financially, and emotionally—to complete their vision. They hauled stone, wove curtains, borrowed money, and argued with authorities.

The steeply gabled building based on a triangle opens out onto its four-acre site in suburban Madison, rather than turning inward as Wright's Unity Temple (1904) did. The expansive, prowlike roof rises from the foyer toward the pulpit, over the bell tower, extending beyond the wall of glass to wide, overhanging eaves. Modular furniture uses the same triangular grammar as the building and can be grouped in rows, circles, or clusters. The foyer, a "hearth room" with a massive walk-in fireplace, can be isolated for more intimate gatherings.

The magnificent copper roof—Wright's answer to the steeple—has recently been restored to ensure that the congregation continues to find shelter there.

In designing a modern Unitarian church building, Frank Lloyd Wright asked a fundamental question. What was the building supposed to express? It must express "unity" was the conclusion.

Rev. Kenneth L. Patton
The Church of Tomorrow, 1947

Instead of defining separate spaces for worship and social activities as in Unity Temple, rooms here were designed to be multifunctional. The main auditorium serves as a living room adaptable for services, meetings, dinners, and concerts. An adjoining wing houses classrooms, offices, and a smaller living room.

MORRIS GIFT SHOP

The ceiling light fixtures are composed of large disks of concave and convex plastic that offer bubbles of light as soft as the discreet markers pointing to the front entrance. The graceful arch recalls fireplaces and other cavelike entries Wright liked to use in his Prairie Style years.

TUCKED AMONG TRADITIONAL STORE-fronts on a narrow urban lane is the treasure box that Wright designed for V. C. Morris. His unconventional but powerful solution for the retail facade is compelling not for its open displays of wares but for the curiosity it stimulates. The simplicity of the high Roman brick wall, broken only by tiny points of light leading to the large asymmetrical entry arch, presents an abstracted cave to explore.

Like earlier retail spaces of Wright's, this was a remodeling. Here, however, he expressed a totally new stylistic grammar that previewed the Guggenheim Museum, completed eleven years later. The exterior restraint explodes inside, the archway giving only a hint of the complex curvilinear composition beyond. A sweeping spiral ramp leads to the upper floor.

Wright fashioned countless special details to maximize the presentation and storage of merchandise. Tiny porthole display spots, intimate viewing corners, even a dumbwaiter for lifting goods all contributed to the functional and artistic harmony. Some of the original fixtures have been removed, but the energy remains.

PRICE TOWER

▦ I think an office building is quite as important as a church and I think it has a function and a feature that can be as beautiful as anything ever built. ▦
Frank Lloyd Wright
"American Forum" (NBC), 1956

Containing only 37,000 square feet in nineteen floors, the Price Tower rises from the plains like a richly adorned, prismatic tree. It took 240 drawings and two years to craft this functional work of art. An integral part of the Bartlesville skyline, the landmark is now owned by Phillips Petroleum.

WRIGHT HAD EXPLORED /KY/CRAPER/ since the mid-1920s, but it took thirty years to find a client ready to build one. Harold Price Sr., an oil pipeline owner, commissioned Wright's tallest building for the plains of Oklahoma. Its taproot concept was a realization of Wright's 1929 St. Mark's Tower scheme for New York.

The Price Tower was another engineering feat using steel in tension, reinforced concrete for the central core, cantilevered floors, extensive glass walls, and prefabricated, stamped-copper louvers and sheathing. Above the broad, two-story base, the dynamic floor plan is a pinwheel within a rotated square. On most floors, three quadrants are triangular and house offices; the fourth is a full square and contains two-story apartments. Top floors hold special office spaces with terraces.

A believer in horizontal lines, Wright found a few tall buildings acceptable if they did not intrude shadows on their neighbors. He used this vertical element in idealized city plans much as he offset his long, low buildings with tall pylons, placing them in free green space, even suggesting a garden for each residence.

BETH SHOLOM SYNAGOGUE

RABBI MORTIMER J. COHEN DREAMED of creating a temple that did not borrow any style but grew from an idea—a truly American synagogue. He and Wright worked together for six years to make this dream a reality. During the same time, Wright was also designing Methodist, Unitarian, Christian Science, Greek Orthodox, and Congregational churches.

Wright was asked to create a soundproof, windowless building using generous amounts of glass for light and air, to place the rabbi in the midst of people, and to make the Torah in the Holy Ark dominant. At least twelve hundred seats were needed plus a chapel for three hundred and other classrooms and meeting rooms.

The temple is an abstraction of two hands turned up in a gesture of offering, a hexagon with two prolongations on either side. To the congregation the shape represented the everlasting hands of God, in which they rest within the synagogue. The symbolism in the inspiring space, portrayed by numerous triangle-based abstractions, completes the dream temple, which rises from the earth like a luminous Mount Sinai.

⊞ The design was radical, an irregular mountain of copper and glass rising more than 100 feet in the air, but even the rabbi's most reluctant board members were awed by the Wright magic and the rabbi's persuasive powers. ⊞

Patricia Talbot Davis
Together They Built
a Mountain, 1974

Wright ultimately gave the congregation outside Philadelphia a tall inverted hexagon using a steel frame, aluminum shells filled with reinforced concrete, outer walls of wired glass, and cream-colored fiberglass inside.

H U M P H R E Y S   T H E A T E R

WRIGHT, THE SHOWMAN, LOVED THE theater, viewing it as another opportunity to present life, to inspire. He began his career working on the Auditorium Theater (1889) for Adler and Sullivan, and he incorporated performance spaces in each of his own three homes, frequently remodeling the one at Taliesin. Over the years he was commissioned to design more than thirty performing arts facilities of various sizes. Despite this interest, his first purely dramatic theater—the Dallas Theater Center space named for Kalita Humphreys—did not come to fruition until the end of his life.

To involve the audience more, to engage them in the performance, he rejected the proscenium as a veritable hole in the wall. In the Humphreys Theater, completed after his death, the stage was round, reached into the audience, and rotated to facilitate easy set changes. The four hundred seats were pulled tightly around it. This central cylindrical form was imbedded in a partially hexagonal building and rose above it. Concentric circular forms rippled in the ceiling, symbolically radiating from the stage to the audience.

❚❚ I would rather solve the small house problem than build anything else I can think of (except the modern theater). ❚❚

Frank Lloyd Wright
Letter to
Architectural Forum, 1938

Reinforced concrete was selected for its malleability and durability—perfect for the circular designs that Wright liked for public buildings. Additions and changes have enclosed the open terrace and paved the grassy hill.

GUGGENHEIM MUSEUM

⠿ We'll have to wait and see how the Guggenheim Museum turns out. But this much is certain: Fifth Avenue, the neighborhood of elegant baroque villas, will never be the same. No neighborhood invaded by Frank Lloyd Wright has ever been the same and that goes for some of his clients as well. ⠿

Morgan Beatty

"Biography in Sound:

Meet Frank Lloyd Wright,"

(NBC), 1956

A major renovation in 1992 added a controversial tower (opposite). The original building (page 46) was restored, including its skylight-topped atrium (page 47).

THE MOST PROLONGED PROJECT OF Wright's career was his commission to design the Guggenheim Museum under the direction of the baroness Hilla Rebay. Commissioned in 1943, it was not completed until 1959, the year he died. The battles with city officials and the engineering and reengineering to satisfy codes, client, and contractor were epic. Wright's final 1956 design, typically unorthodox, challenged the capacity of cantilevers to sustain massive amounts of cast concrete.

Early sketches showed a hexagonal design as well as a circular version of an ancient ziggurat, with each floor smaller than the one below. The ultimate spiral design, however, is inverted, larger at the top than the bottom, and features an interior ramp that gradually unwinds within the cone-shaped central gallery. Patrons are encouraged to ride the elevator to the top of the building and leisurely follow the curved path to the bottom, passing the naturally lighted art along the way.

The sculptural fluidity of the design suited the plasticity of concrete. It is a masterful execution of the circular forms that dominated Wright's later work.

ANNUNCIATION GREEK ORTHODOX CHURCH

WAUWATOSA, WISCONSIN. 1956

⚏ This looked to me like the dome was the church, and yet it was utilitarian at the same time. When you hear of seating a thousand people in a church with no pillars to obstruct your vision . . . , this impressed me a lot. This is what *ekklesia* means in Greek, you know: you are part of the group. ⚏
Stanley Stacey
Annunciation Building Committee, 1986

Wright cleverly united the two ancient symbols of the church, the cross and the circle, and provided large but intimate and inspirational spaces the church sought.

WHEN WRIGHT DESIGNED THIS SAUCER-shaped church, he openly drew on Byzantine architectural forms while creating a modern work of art "dedicated to ancient Tradition instead of living upon it." Wright was asked to consider traditional Greek Orthodox cruciform plans, barrel vaults, and domes and to provide seating for seven hundred. His shocking response was a giant, shallow domed lid over a gently curved bowl that rests in a cradle shaped like a Greek cross.

The interaction of the two geometric forms continues inside, with a sweep of curved balcony surrounding the central space. Everything follows suit: bold architectural forms, a shallow-arched entry, an arcade of art glass windows, a visor encircling the dome, Greek crosses incised in concrete columns, round urns on square bases, and curved garden walls. Masses of tiny crosses within circles create a golden fretwork screen around the altar; small glass spheres on crosses form columns of light; circular forms in polychromatic icons repeat the theme. Budgeted at $500,000, the church ultimately cost $1.5 million when completed five years later.

Four massive piers hold the blue-roofed disk aloft, where it hovers over an underground complex of meeting rooms. Low urns outside mirror the building's shape itself and resemble some of the architect's earliest ornamental devices from decades before.

MARIN COUNTY CIVIC CENTER

The radio and television tower (above) adds a vertical accent to the curvy horizontality, while a barrel-vaulted atrium (opposite) offers natural light. Rhythmic rows of sand-colored arches of cast concrete (pages 54–55) stretch beneath a giant blue roof.

WHEN THE NINETY-YEAR-OLD WRIGHT first visited the site of the Marin County Civic Center, he conceived a horizontal building that would bridge its picturesque hills, embracing them. His only civic building built to date became a sweep of long curved forms, drawing again on the circle for its architectural language.

Bringing all county government functions under one roof, Wright produced flexible open areas, free of columns and divided by movable anodized aluminum panels. First came the elliptical, concrete-block post office. The four-story concrete and steel Administration Building, stuck for a time in a political quagmire, houses the board of supervisors and library and is 584 feet long with an eighty-foot diameter dome. The larger wing, the Hall of Justice, completed in 1969, is 880 feet long and contains courtrooms, offices, and the jail. Each level has an open core that gets larger near the top and is capped by an acrylic skylight.

With Wright's death in 1959, the construction depended greatly on the working drawings and supervision of Aaron Green and the Taliesin Associated Architects.

Davis, Patricia Talbot. *Together They Built a Mountain*. Lititz, Pa.: Sutter House, 1974.

Dunham, Judith. *Details of Frank Lloyd Wright: The California Work, 1909–1974*. San Francisco: Chronicle, 1994.

Green, Aaron G. *An Architecture for Democracy: The Marin County Civic Center*. San Francisco: Grendon Publishing, 1990.

Gurda, John. *New World Odyssey: Annunciation Greek Orthodox Church and Frank Lloyd Wright*. Milwaukee: Milwaukee Hellenic Community, 1986.

Hamilton, Mary Jane. *The Meeting House Heritage and Vision*. Madison: Friends of the Meeting House, 1991.

Lipman, Jonathan. *Frank Lloyd Wright and the Johnson Wax Buildings*. New York: Rizzoli, 1986.

Manson, Grant Carpenter. *Frank Lloyd Wright to 1910*. New York: Van Nostrand Reinhold, 1958.

Pfeiffer, Bruce Brooks, ed. *Frank Lloyd Wright: Monographs. 1887–1959*. Vols. 1–8. Tokyo: ADA Edita, 1985–88.

Pfeiffer, Bruce Brooks, and Gerald Nordlan, eds. *Frank Lloyd Wright: In the Realm of Ideas*. Carbondale: Southern Illinois University Press, 1988.

Universes of circles—spheres and portholes, lamps and circuitous ramps—populate the interior of the Morris Gift Shop (1948) in downtown San Francisco. Wright's austere facade belies the explosion of sensuous forms inside.

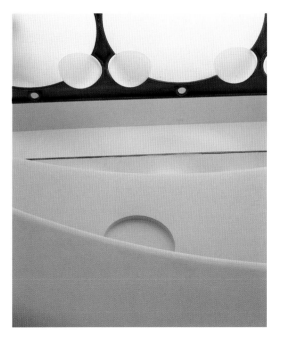

Illustration Sources:

© Farrell Grehan:

10, 15 top left, 15 bottom left, 15 bottom right, 22, 23, 24, 25, 26, 27, 29, 30, 30–31, 51

© Scott Frances/Esto: 54–55

© Jeff Goldberg/Esto: 2, 45, 47

© Pedro E. Guerrero: 1, 33

Historic American Buildings Survey:

17 (Allan Steenhusen); 41 (Jack E. Boucher)

© Balthazar Korab:

6–7, 8, 11, 15 top right, 16, 18, 19, 32, 34–35, 38, 42, 46, 48, 50–51, 52

© Steinkamp/Ballogg Chicago:

21 (James Steinkamp)

© Scot Zimmerman:

12, 13, 36, 37, 53, 57